# HERIZON

story by: Daniel W. Vandever
illustrated by: Corey Begay

© 2021 South of Sunrise Creative

Library of Congress Cataloging-in-Publication Data

Names: Vandever, Daniel W., author, Corey Begay, illustrator.
Title: Herizon / story by Daniel W. Vandever and illustrated by Corey Begay
Description: First edition. | Grants, New Mexico : South of Sunrise Creative,
[2021] | Summary: A young Diné girl helps her grandmother retrieve a flock of
sheep with a magical scarf that transforms the world she knows.

Identifiers:  Library of Congress Control Number: 2021913641
            ISBN 9781737496403
Subjects: | Children's Fiction | Curiosities and Wonders


Layout by Daniel W. Vandever
Designed by Corey Begay

Printed in the United States of America

First Printing, First Edition

South of Sunrise Creative
Grants, New Mexico 87020
www.southofsunrisecreative.com

To my nieces:

Your horizon has no limit.

Be bold. Be beautiful. Be you.

Love,
Uncle Dan

Characters, setting, and transitions help guide a story with no words. Use the symbols below to help navigate *Herizon* and better understand the growth of the main character. Readers may use the questions matching each symbol to help guide discussion.

**C** **CHARACTER** – What is the character thinking? How does the character feel? Can you describe a time you felt like this?

**S** **SETTING** – Where does the scene take place? What does it tell you about the character(s)? Why is it important?

**T** **TRANSITION** – What is happening in the sequence? How does it represent growth? What do you think will happen next?

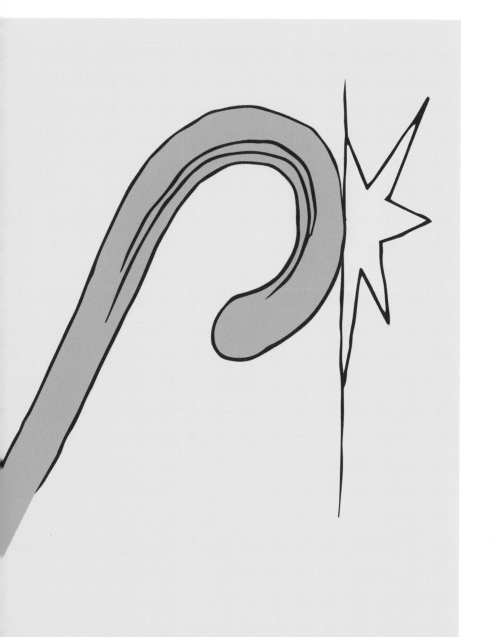

T

c

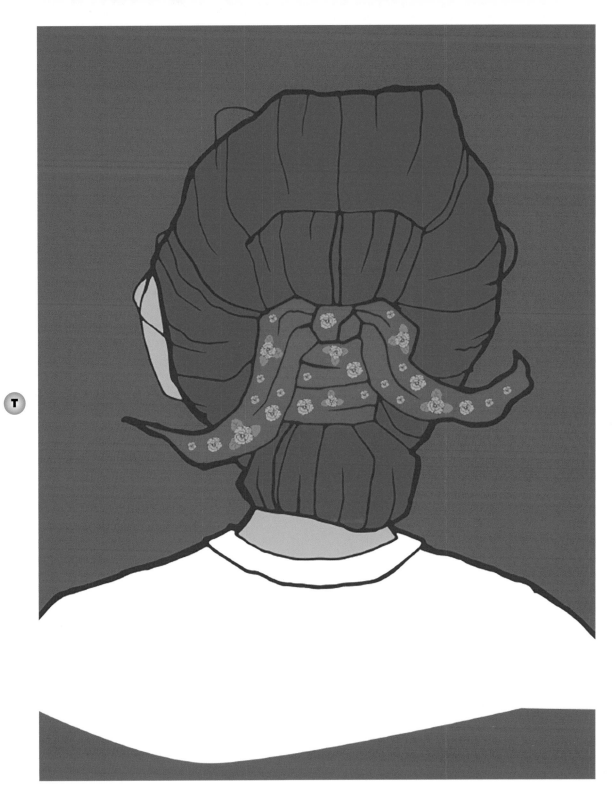

Navajo Bun/Tsiiyéél

# #HERIZON

Join the *Herizon* movement!
Post a picture of your Sáanii
Scarf designs to social media.

Learn more about
*Herizon* by scanning
the QR code with your
smart phone camera.

The girl comes of age when her
grandmother ties her hair in a Navajo bun.

Scarf/Ch'ah or
Zéédéeltsoozí

The scarf represents intergenerational
strength and knowledge. It is red
in honor of Missing and Murdered
Indigenous Relatives.

Hair/Atsii'

Growth is represented by the girl's hair;
from wild and unruly to fixed and poised.

## AUTHOR'S NOTE

*Herizon* is a story of female empowerment and intergenerational strength. Females are at the center of Diné (Navajo) worldview as identity is determined through one's mother. As such, females are sacred beings that bear life, nurture growth, and provide safety and security within the home and community. The role of nurturer was taught by the diety Changing Woman, who over time, had her teachings systematically attacked through strategies like boarding school era education and legislation intended to dismantle the family unit.

But we are resilient, and our identity and values have persisted. As the Navajo Nation moves forward, it is our mothers, sisters, aunts, grandmas, wives, and daughters that will help us thrive in the modern world. As a son, brother, uncle, and grandson, I lend my encouragement in supporting efforts for equal opportunities and equitable rights. For the sake of my nieces and the future of the Navajo Nation, it is a responsibility to serve as an advocate with books like *Herizon*.

## THEMES/IMAGERY

The below images had larger meaning than what was depicted in the story. Can you go back and find them in the book?

Dish Towel/
Łeets'aah
bee yit'oodí

The dish towel represents
traditional female roles.

Butterfly/
K'aalógii

Insects helped Navajos ascend
from the first world into present
time. The butterflies represent
the start of the girl's journey.

Cousins/
Shizeedí

The girl's cousins represent laziness.

Sheep/Dibé

The sheep represent traditional
Navajo lifeways.

Spider Rock/
Tsé na'ashjé'ii

Spider Rock, home of
the diety Spider Woman,
revives the girl's spirit
after facing setbacks of
falling off her horse and
confronting a waterfall.

## DISCUSSION GUIDE

Now that you've read *Herizon*, see if you can answer these questions. The questions are according to principles of the Diné philosophy of learning: *Nitsáhákees, Nahatá, Iiná,* and *Sihasin*.

### 1. Nitsáhákees (Thinking)

1. What was the story about?
2. Who are the characters?
3. Where did the story take place?
4. When did the story take place?

### 2. Nahatá (Planning)

1. What was the conflict of the story?
2. How did it make the girl feel? Why?
3. What was special about grandma's scarf?
4. Why is it important to help our elders?

### 3. Iiná (Implementation)

1. How did the girl grow throughout the story?
2. What challenges did the girl face?
3. How was the conflict resolved?
4. Why is it important to never give up?

### 4. Sihasin (Reflection)

1. What was your favorite part of the book?
2. Have you ever felt like the girl? When?
3. Was the story real or just the girl's imagination?
4. What is on the girl's horizon? What is next?

Coyote/Mą'ii

Threats to traditional Navajo lifeways are
represented by the coyotes.

Window Rock/
Tséghahoodzání

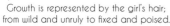

The final image in the story respresents the
Navajo Nation's future and female representation
in government, healthcare, energy, and business.